9 Months of Happiness:

PREGNANCY JOURNAL

•••

Maintaining a Blissful Pregnancy

YouAreCreators
P.O. Box 756
Tinley Park, IL 60477

ISBN-10: 0692650008
ISBN-13: 978-0692650004

First Edition

Dedication:

Mothers

You are POWERFUL BEINGS.

This Journal Belongs To:

_____

The Day My Pregnancy Journey Begin:

_____

1st Trimester

" The beginning of something special…"

Date_____

Date_____

Date_____

_____

_____

_____

_____

Did You Know?
In the 1950's the
word "pregnant" was
too vulgar for TV so
they used
euphemisms like,
"expecting" instead?

_____

_____

_____

_____

_____

_____

_____

_____

_____

Date_____

Date_____

Date_____

Date_____

Date_____

Date_____

Date_____

" Everyday may not be easy but, you can do this."

Date_____

Date_____

Date_____

Date_____

_____

_____

Did You Know?
Pregnant women
and new mothers
can lactate when
they hear the sound
of a crying baby?

_____

_____

_____

_____

_____

_____

_____

_____

_____

_____

Date_____

Date_____

Date_____

Date_____

Pregnancy Affirmations:

Affirmations are statements used that allow you to consciously control your thoughts.

The repetition of affirmations can positively impact the way that you feel and increase mental stability.

Here are a few helpful affirmations to use during your pregnancy, feel free to add some of your own. Remember, baby can hear these too!

1. I am healthy, strong and powerful.

2. My body is amazing and capable of developing a healthy baby.

3. I can do this!

Date_____

Date_____

Date_____

Date_____

Date_____

Date_____

Date_____

7 Things That Make Me Happy...

1. _____

2. _____

3. _____

4. _____

5. _____

6. _____

7. _____

Date_____

Date_____

Date_____

Date_____

Date_____

Blissful Tip:

"Instead of focusing on feeling ill, redirect your attention to the visualization of how your baby's little face will look.

It'll all be worth it, in the end..."

Date_____

Date_____

Date_____

Date_____

Date_____

Date_____

Date_____

Date_____

Date_____

Date_____

Date_____

Date_____

Date_____

Blissful Tip:

"Playing music (especially classical or gentle harmonious music) is a great way to elevate your mood and relax. Baby's little ears can hear the gentle sounds as well (beginning week 18)."

Date_____

Date_____

Date_____

Date_____

_____

_____

_____

_____

Did You Know?
During pregnancy,
your uterus
expands to about
500 times its
normal size?

Date_____

Date_____

Date_____

2nd Trimester

"You're doing it, you're going to

be an amazing mommy…"

Date_____

Date_____

Date_____

Date_____

Date_____

Date_____

Date_____

Date_____

Date_____

" Right Now, Your Body is Actively
Creating a Miracle."

Date_____

Date_____

Date_____

Date_____

Date_____

7 Things That Make Me Happy...

1. _____

2. _____

3. _____

4. _____

5. _____

6. _____

7. _____

Date_____

Date_____

Date_____

Date_____

Date_____

Date_____

Date_____

Date_____

Date_____

Date_____

_____

_____

_____

_____

_____

_____

_____

_____

_____

_____

_____

_____

_____

Date_____

<u>Blissful Tip:</u>

"Take a break, breathe deep, smile for no reason, rub your belly, and imagine seeing those little toes…

Your body was wonderfully designed to grow life within…"

Date_____

Date_____

Date_____

Date_____

Date_____

Date_____

Date_____

Date_____

Date_____

Date_____

Date_____

<u>Blissful Tip:</u>

"Treat yourself! Doesn't have to be anything fancy but rewarding yourself is a great way to bring a little joy to your life. You are so worth it and deserve to spoil yourself a little."

Date_____

Date_____

Date_____

Date_____

Date_____

Date_____

_____

_____

_____

_____

_____

_____

_____

_____

_____

_____

_____

_____

Date_____

Date_____

Date_____

Date_____

Date_____

Date_____

Date_____

3rd Trimester

"You're almost there, beautiful…"

Date_____

Date_____

Date_____

Date_____

Date_____

Date_____

Date_____

_____

_____

_____

_____

_____

_____

_____

_____

_____

_____

_____

_____

Date_____

Date_____

"During your pregnancy you have the
opportunity to not only influence
your mood, but your unborn child as
well..."

Date_____

Date_____

Date_____

Date_____

Date_____

Date_____

Date_____

Date_____

Date_____

Date_____

Date_____

7 Things That Make Me Happy...

1. _____

2. _____

3. _____

4. _____

5. _____

6. _____

7. _____

Date_____

_____

_____

_____

_____

_____

_____

_____

_____

_____

_____

_____

_____

Date_____

Date_____

Date_____

Date_____

Date_____

Date_____

Date_____

Date_____

Blissful Tip:

"Running water has negative ions, negative ions create positive vibes. A nice warm shower or bath and/or a refreshing glass of water can help improve your mood when feeling down."

Date_____

Date_____

Date_____

Date_____

Date_____

Date_____

Date_____

Date_____

Date_____

Date_____

_____

_____

_____

_____

Did You Know?
The longest
pregnancy on
record lasted 375
days!

_____

_____

_____

_____

_____

_____

_____

_____

Date_____

Date_____

Date_____

Date_____

Date_____

Gratitude Exercise:

Gratitude is so important in creating a fulfilling life. Happiness is truly achieved when we can appreciate even the little things in our life. Below, jot down 5 things that you are grateful for. These things can serve as a reminder for you when you're feeling down.

1. _____

2. _____

3. _____

4. _____

5. _____

Date_____

Date_____

Date_____

Meditation Tips:

Meditating can help slow things down.
Learning to control your breathing and
relax is essential to giving birth. Here
are a few tips to help.

1. Find a comfortable, quiet space.

2. Position yourself into a comfortable
posture.

3. Relax your eyes, closing your eyes
work best.

4. Inhale deeply, exhale slowly.

5. Empty your mind, and allow yourself to
relax more with each breath.

Baby's Birthday:

_____

Baby's Name:

_____

Congratulations!